The New GATEKEEPERS

CENSORING CHRISTIANS IN THE DIGITAL AGE

The New GATEKEEPERS

CENSORING CHRISTIANS IN THE DIGITAL AGE

D. JAMES KENNEDY MINISTRIES

D. JAMES
KENNEDY
MINISTRIES

Fort Lauderdale, FL

The New Gatekeepers
Censoring Christians in the Digital Age

Copyright © 2018 D. James Kennedy Ministries

Unless otherwise indicated, Scripture quotations are taken from *The Holy Bible, English Standard Version*, copyright © 2001 by Crossway Bibles, a ministry of Good News Publishers. All rights reserved. Used by permission.

ISBN: 978-1-929626-82-3

Cover and Interior Design: Roark Creative, www.roarkcreative.com

Printed in the United States of America.

Published by:

D. James Kennedy Ministries
P.O. Box 11786
Fort Lauderdale, FL 33339
1-800-988-7884
DJKM.org
letters@djkm.org

CONTENTS

INTRODUCTION

MEET THE GATEKEEPERS

We have all experienced it. You search for something on the internet—let's say a new dishwasher. The next thing you know, advertisements for appliances start to pop up interrupting your every internet interaction. You sign on to Facebook, and there's a sponsored ad or suggested post about dishwashers. You visit a website and an ad pops up that invites, *"For the best price on name brand appliances, click here!"* It's as if someone is reading your mind.

Technology is watching.

In recent years, however, Big Technology—specifically the big four: *Google, Amazon, Facebook,* and *Apple*—have moved beyond just culling your digital habits and history in order to market products and services to you. They have been quietly establishing themselves as information and media *"gatekeepers,"* attempting to control the flow of knowledge and information we see, and thereby influence—if not completely manipulate—national and global discourse.

Consider how these four companies have positioned themselves, and how we, as consumers, have unwittingly anointed their rise.

Google is the "go-to" for information searches

The moniker has, for all intents and purposes, become a verb: *"Just google it."* Where past generations spent hours in libraries poring over card catalogs and piling up reference books, today's students surf, point, and click. Where we once turned to print and broadcast journalism for insights, contextualization, and analysis of the world's happenings, today we're receiving alerts and push-notifications, all but shouting to us, *"This is urgent! Give this your attention, now!"*

In the summer of 2015, Google renamed itself Alphabet. Their search engine is still called Google, but now they are about so much more. Their reach has extended into internet infrastructure, software, hardware, browsers, telephones, advertising, social media, home electronics, education, television and video production, maps and GPS locator services—even self-driving automobiles. That's just scratching the surface. Alphabet subsidiaries reach even further, into social, economic, and political realms. In simple terms, this tech giant is seeking to become the world's portal to information and knowledge.

Alphabet/Google's ultimate project is AI—artificial intelligence. Google wants to create machines that can function like—or, more specifically, function beyond—the human brain. Further still, they aim to effectively weld this artificial brain to humans. In other words: Google will do the thinking—for you and me.

Amazon has redefined where and how we shop

Books were just the beginning. What started as *Earth's Largest Bookstore* in the 1990s has become *Earth's Largest Everything Store.* It is not a stretch to say Amazon forever changed the way consumers behave. Running an errand has been replaced by going online. Amazon paved the e-commerce highway. One-click ordering, Prime shipping, and door-to-door delivery with package tracking with email or text notifications—because we all need to know, "*Your Amazon order left the distribution center this morning at 4:49 a.m. It's out for delivery today at 3:22 p.m.*"

Amazon is taking writers and publishers to the woodshed. They have been so successful, they have been able to position themselves so that old media must depend on their platform to reach their audience. If you want to go to market, you must play by Amazon's rules.

When you, the consumer, buy a book from Amazon—for convenience sake, yes, but also because brick-and-mortar booksellers are shuttering at an alarming rate—you are offered other suggested titles, related products, and deals. You've seen it: *Customers who bought this item also bought . . .*" In other words, "*We think you will like . . .*" and cha-ching! That's just good sales strategy, you say?

Yes. But it's more.

Amazon doesn't just publish books and produce television shows and movies. They want to have all media—sight, sound, and word—under one umbrella. As one of the new media gatekeepers, Amazon sees a day in the future when there is only one gate. Theirs.

So, while this exposé is about how the new gatekeepers are censoring *information*, another could be written about their dominance beyond media. Amazon's reach now extends to just about all product lines and impacts almost every producer. If you sell widgets, you had better get them listed on Amazon. The world won't come to your door. But Amazon *is* in every home, and you can tell "Alexa," Amazon's virtual digital assistant, *"Order me a widget."* But, as many niche producers have experienced, when Amazon's machinery finds an especially profitable widget, they may decide to manufacture their own version. Like old media and brick-and-mortar booksellers, niche producers' days are numbered.

Facebook is where we socialize

It is the town square for social debate, the meeting place for sharing, having fun and playing games, and the "water cooler" where we meet for everything from small-talk to major whining and complaining. Think it. Post it. Like it. Share it. Comment on it. And just like that—*Where has the last hour gone?*

What creator Mark Zuckerberg started as an internet bulletin board for Ivy League student hook-ups has exploded into a global cyber community. It's where your friends are—by hundreds or even thousands more than the friends you physically see in passing. It's become our portal into one another's lives, and it has cultivated a population of voyeurs. Facebook has become an hours-a-day, every day obsession—and yes, for many, even an addiction.

Beyond social interaction, Facebook has become a hub for social action and even extremism. People are finding their voice—and it's not always good—organizing with others in alliance with or opposition to the latest cause du jour. Crowdsourcing and event invites carry tremendous potential and reach. Media of all kinds and expressions come to life in people's news feed, prompting a direct response.

Apple is where we turn for entertainment

It didn't start out that way. When Steve Jobs, Steve Wozniak, and Ronald Wayne got together in the mid-seventies, it was about one thing—marketing Wozniak's Apple I personal computer. Within a few years, they'd added a small staff of employees. Innovation was their niche—they *thought differently* in response to IBM's slogan of 'Think.'

Apple's stable today includes quite a range of products: computers and laptops, phones, tablets, watches, operating systems, software products, home entertainment products, iTunes, Apple Stores, the App Store, iCloud, and more—and a cult-like audience of millions anxiously await the next Apple Event to see which frontiers they'll conquer next.

While these giants create the impression that they are offering us choice and championing individualism, they're actually nudging you and me—all of us—in the direction they want to move us. Google, Amazon, Facebook, and Apple believe they know what is best for you, and they are actively engaged in transporting you there.

The stealth engines driving these gatekeepers' ascension are *algorithms.* By simple definition, an algorithm is *a process or set of rules to be followed in calculations or other problem-solving operations, especially by a computer.* Ponder that definition for just a moment and you will see the revolutionary potential within it. Algorithms were created to automate thinking. They are said to remove human fallibility and be free of all bias and emotion. Simple mechanized steps—like a recipe—yielding *the right outcome.*

The work of algorithms goes on unseen. In other words, you have not filled out any survey that says you would like to see more advertisements for appliances or more news from a particular market or niche. They work behind the scenes, silently watching, gathering, interpreting, and acting.

Algorithms constantly measure us and make decisions based on those measurements. And this is key—they make those decisions seemingly *on our behalf.* The algorithm sees you are looking for a new dishwasher. It determines your need to see ads about new kitchen appliances right now, and *voila!* It sees you often "like" pictures of puppies—and you realize there have been *a lot* of pictures of puppies in your feed. Coincidence? It notices you frequent Boston sports sites and follow the Boston Red Sox page, and you realize you're seeing more sports, more of every Boston franchise . . . and no mentions of the New York Yankees in your feed. They've got you measured. They are simply aiding in offering you your own preferences. *They decide that's what you want.* Convenient, yes?

They're watching. And they're constantly testing: *What do you like? Dislike? What do you click on? What do you ignore? What do you crave?* Facebook boasts that they can predict users' race, sexual orientation, relationship status, and drug use *all simply based on "likes" alone.* As Star Trek's Mr. Spock would say, "It's logical deduction. The sum of the data."

But what if an algorithm is created to reflect the values of its creator? What if they are used to tinker with how you and I—everyone—view the world? What if Big Tech and its left-of-left leaning CEOs, board members, and technicians determine to reshape your worldview?

In this way, algorithms are being employed today by Big Tech to *erode free will* and *undermine free speech.* They are purported to be lightening our burden. In reality, they're moving us in someone else's preferred direction. And here is the truly chilling part of it—*we're almost entirely unaware that it is happening.*

This exposé takes a deeper look at the Big Tech Gatekeepers, their motives, methods, and manipulations. We will look at several egregious examples of their conduct in binding free will and stifling free speech. We will also look at the tremendous inconsistency these tech giants employ in practices that clearly contradict their stated neutrality and expose their left-leaning agendas.

In addition, we will consider the threat this intrusion and manipulation poses to our rights and our freedoms. Finally, we'll explore options: What can we do? How can we protect ourselves, our privacy, our values, and our future?

Big Tech believes they know what is best for us all and they are only too happy to steer us onto their preferred path toward what they consider to be an enlightened future. But in truth, that path is one that would lead to tyranny and subjugation—especially of Christians and the message of Christ.

Let's take a closer look.

CHAPTER 1

EGREGIOUS GATEKEEPING EXAMPLES

"The biggest tech companies are, among other things, the most powerful gatekeepers the world has ever known."

—**Franklin Foer**, Author, *World Without Mind*[1]

CENSORED

Conservatives recognized hostile attempts by liberals to quiet, if not quell, conservative voices and viewpoints through Clinton-era attempts to reenact selected portions of the *fairness doctrine*. The same happened in Obama-era regulations imposed under the guise of *net neutrality*. As those bids were turned back, a new and even greater potential threat to the freedoms of speech and expression emerged in the form of giant tech corporations headed by liberal CEOs and executives—they took up the effort, and began discriminating against viewpoints they dislike.

What else can be deduced from the growing list of egregious examples of stunningly one-sided, no rhyme nor reason, heavy-handed procedural and editorial assaults against conservatives expressing their views?

What are we talking about? Let these briefs give you a taste:

- Facebook suspended the account of a ministry known as *Warriors for Christ* because their page, by stating homosexuality and abortion are sins, *"violates Facebook's community standards on bullying and hate speech."*[2] Yet, when a conservative blogger known by the moniker *Activist Mommy* discovered a pro-homosexual Facebook group named *"I Will Find the Activist Mommy and Burn Whoever Runs It Alive"* and reported it to Facebook, she was informed the page *"doesn't violate our Community Standards.*[3]

- A fact-check widget appeared in the sidebar of Google's search results for a handful of conservative sites and publications like *Daily Caller*. At the same time, no such fact-check treatment was proffered for known left-leaning sites and publications like *Vox, Slate, Huffington Post*, or *Mother Jones*.[4]

- Pro-life organization *Human Coalition* had its 5-star rated *pro-life prayer application* dropped from Apple's App Store after Apple received criticism and complaints from pro-abortion activists and liberal-leaning media.[5]

- *Heritage Foundation* senior research fellow Ryan Anderson saw his book, *When Harry Became Sally*, skyrocket to the top of Amazon's Gay and Lesbian Civil Rights bestseller list. Complaints poured in, like this tweet from LBGT activist/journalist Matt Baume, *"Amazon is giving credibility to an anti-trans book by allowing it to gurgle its way up to the #1 spot in the category of Gay & Lesbian Civil Rights History, a place it could not possibly deserve less to be."* Amazon removed Anderson's book from the Gay & Lesbian Civil Rights bestseller list, but kept it on its Natural Law bestseller list.[6]

With these few examples, we're only scratching the surface. The time has come to take the threat each of these tech giant gatekeepers poses more seriously. With *Google—the portal to knowledge; Amazon—the starting point to all commerce; Facebook—the online neighborhood of some two billion;* and *Apple—the master of all digital downloads,* we need to be aware and cautious of their aims, actions, methods, and manipulations. These firms tell us they are out to make the world a better place. But be concerned. Their definition of a better place differs dramatically and significantly from yours.

> The time has come to take the threat each of these tech giant gatekeepers poses more seriously.

Franklin Foer says it well in his book, *World Without Mind: The Existential Threat of Big Tech*:

> The big tech companies—and the Europeans have charmingly, and correctly lumped them together as GAFA (Google, Apple, Facebook, Amazon)—are shredding the principles that protect individuality. Their devices and sites have collapsed privacy; they disrespect the value of authorship, with their hostility to intellectual property. In the realm of economics, they justify monopoly with their well-articulated belief that competition undermines our pursuit of the common good and ambitious goals. When it comes to the most central tenet of individualism—free will—the tech companies have a different way. They hope to automate the choices, both large and small, that we make as we float through the day. It's their algorithms that suggest the news we read, the goods we buy, the path we travel, the friends we invite into our circle.[7]

CHAPTER 2

Alphabet/Google: "Do the Right Thing"

"Sergey and I founded Google because we're super optimistic about the potential for technology to make the world a better place."

—**Larry Page**, Co-Founder, Alphabet CEO

"We want Google to be the third half of your brain."

—**Sergey Brin**, Co-Founder, Alphabet President

Back in the days when people thought personal computers were just a passing fad, Carl Page brought an Exidy Sorcerer computer home to his sons, Carl, Jr., and Larry. The brothers wrote an operating system for their new toy. With homemade software and a dot-matrix printer, Larry decided one day to type up his homework. It was the first time anyone at his school had ever seen a printed assignment.

Carl Page, Sr., died in 1996. Larry came across his father's high school valedictory speech, delivered in 1956, and shares of the discovery, "I was blown away." In the speech, his father had asserted, *"We shall take part in, or witness, developments in science, medicine, and industry that we cannot dream of today."* Larry adopted his father's dream. He articulated his part in the bigger picture in the initial mission statement of Google: *"Our mission is to organize the world's information and make it universally accessible and useful."*[8]

When Larry Page and Sergey Brin birthed the search engine Google while they were Ph.D. students at Stanford University, they did so creating algorithms that would replicate—and at least where speed and accuracy were concerned, outperform—the human brain. Page and Brin imagined going even further. As Brin has said, the goal was for this artificial intelligence to one day function as "the third half of your brain."

When Alphabet/Google talks about reshaping the future, they are not simply talking about convenience; Alphabet/Google is intent on imposing its values on the world.

Take the aforementioned instance of Google gatekeeping—*assigning fact-checking widgets to searches for conservative sites and publications, but not those of a liberal bent.* That should be worrisome enough. But the partisanship runs deeper. Google's roster of supposedly neutral, third-party fact-check providers includes so-called objective sources like Snopes, Climate Feedback, and even the Southern Poverty Law Center

> Alphabet/Google is intent on imposing its values on the world.

(SPLC). Perhaps you recall the SPLC's branding of D. James Kennedy Ministries, the American Family Association, and other similar family-friendly ministries and organizations as *hate groups* for their traditional Christian views? Yes, *that SPLC* is helping to fact-check your web search results. Doesn't that knowledge inspire confidence?

> Not only is Google's fact-checking highly partisan—many of the results these fact-checks reported have been wrong.

Not only is Google's fact-checking highly partisan—perhaps reflecting the views of its leaders—but as you have probably imagined by now, many of the *results* these fact-checks have reported are wrong.

For example, an article about Robert Mueller and his special counsel's oversight of the investigation into Russia's meddling in the 2016 United States presidential election and related matters mentioned that he had hired a Hillary Clinton donor to assist in the investigation of the Trump Campaign. The fact-check assigned to this article stated, "the claim that Robert Mueller is hiring all Hillary Clinton supporters is false." Yes—if that were what the article had claimed. But the article in question contained no such language asserting the investigation into the Trump Administration and Russia is entirely comprised of Clinton donors. A little exaggeration? Or is it manipulation?

In another example, Snopes, the organization that styles itself in its Twitter bio as an *"investigator of urban legends, rumors, hoaxes, and all manner of codswallop,"* determined a news piece by *The Daily Caller* was "a mixture" of fact and fiction. The claim made, according to Snopes.com—and thereby, also Google—is that *The Daily Caller* reported *"a transgender woman raped a young girl in a women's bathroom because bills were passed . . ."* There's a glaring problem with this claim and review. If you read the news item in question, there is no mention of a bill or any form of legislation whatsoever. The story was simply a straightforward reporting of a disturbing incident that had occurred. In other words, a fact-check of the Snopes claim itself showed it was fiction. Google presented it to you as fact.[9]

Rest assured, the very definition of fact—a thing indisputable—can become lost when arguing radical ideology or worldview. Another of those helpful *reviewed claims* made by *The Daily Caller* was that *climate models used by proponents of climate change*—until recently called global warming—*overestimate the sensitivity of climate to carbon dioxide*. The fact-check determined this is *incorrect*. The supposedly objective fact-checker on this? Climate Feedback—a group of scientists known to fall strongly on one side of the debate. Yet, a healthy a portion of the scientific community would agree with the *Daily Caller's* claim. In other words, this isn't a matter beyond dispute. But Google is happy to stick a fork in it for you.

It is in this way—and in others just as concerning—that Alphabet/Google is seeking to "*organize the world's information and make it universally accessible and useful.*"

The world experienced a glimpse behind the curtain when James Damore, a Google engineer, was fired for circulating a memo criticizing the company's diversity policies in August of 2017. Damore filed a class-action lawsuit. In it, he described a corporate culture in which managers and employees conspire to stifle conservative views and retaliate against conservative employees, all while implementing race-and-gender-based hiring and advancement criteria that may be unlawful.

The complaint opens with this description:

> *Google employees and managers strongly preferred to hear the same orthodox opinions regurgitated repeatedly, producing an ideological echo chamber, a protected, distorted bubble of groupthink. When Plaintiffs challenged Google's illegal employment practices, they were openly threatened and subjected*

to harassment and retaliation from Google. Google created an environment of protecting employees who harassed individuals who spoke out against Google's view or the "Googley way," as it is sometimes known internally. Google employees knew they could harass Plaintiffs with impunity, given the tone set by managers—and they did so.[10]

Let's take a step back. What, specifically did Damore say in the memo? Here are some direct quotes:

- "We need to stop assuming that gender gaps imply sexism. Discrimination to reach equal representation is unfair, divisive, and bad for business."

- "Google's political bias has equated the freedom from offense with psychological safety, but shaming into silence is the antithesis of psychological safety."

- "This silencing has created an ideological echo chamber where some ideas are too sacred to be honestly discussed."

- "Political orientation is actually a result of deep moral preferences and thus biases. Considering that the overwhelming majority of the social sciences, media, and Google lean left, we should critically examine these prejudices."

"Portions of [Damore's] memo violate our code of conduct and cross the line by advancing harmful gender stereotypes in our workplace," said Google CEO Sundar Pichai in a company-wide email after Damore's termination.

> Alphabet/
> Google is
> about more
> than organizing
> the world's
> information.
> They're actively
> attending and
> controlling
> the world's
> information as
> a gatekeeper.

At the time of this writing, other conservative former Google employees are joining this lawsuit, each with their own disturbing experiences to share. Bonuses awarded through peer-to-peer recognition of "speaking up for Googley values"; blocking colleagues with conservative social or political views on company social media and communication platforms; the blacklisting of conservative employees where advancement or transfer opportunities are concerned—the list of egregious behavior is growing.

It's pretty clear, Alphabet/Google is about more than *organizing the world's information*. They're actively *attending and controlling the world's information as a gatekeeper*. Ask Pamela Geller, president of the American Freedom Defense Initiative. Recently, after ProPublica, a George Soros funded "think tank" put out a hit piece on Geller, she noticed her website disappeared from Google searches, and she was banned from Google AdSense. (PayPal suspended her account, also.)[11]

Geller is clear. It's her belief this is an attack on the First Amendment: *"This is a systematic takedown of conservative websites. . . . Never . . . in recent history, has so much power, immense power, been in the hands of so few."*

Amazon: "Earth's Most Customer-Centric Company"

"I want to see good financial returns, but also to me there's the extra psychic return of having my creativity and technological vision bear fruit and change the world in a positive way."

—**Jeff Bezos**, Founder and CEO, Amazon

CENSORED

Jeff Bezos graduated with degrees in electrical engineering and computer science from Princeton University in 1986. He eventually ended up working with a hedge-fund where his responsibilities blended technology and finance. He rose in the organization to become a vice president tasked with "exploring new business opportunities in the burgeoning world of the internet." A rising star was born.

Bezos recognized the internet was changing the world. He grappled with the notion that before consumers would fully acclimate to online shopping, they'd need an on-ramp, a gateway product to ease their way in. Books, he determined, would be a perfect bridge. Books have pretty set costs, and were easy to acquire. Readers order books and rarely return them. And delivery—books are just about indestructible in shipping. He had the perfect plan. Amazon was born in 1994.

Referred to as the *Earth's Largest Bookstore*, Bezos's Amazon had no shelves or warehouses. Instead, he built relationships with big book distributors and built a network like the publishing world had never imagined. With the advent of the internet, knowledge had never been so easily accessible—point and click. Bezos heard the music: point, click, profit. He also saw the future: a monopoly on knowledge.

The new frontier—this inexhaustibly vast store of knowledge known as the internet—would require some mechanism for searching that was much more efficient than the old card catalogs in libraries or walking the aisles at a brick-and-mortar bookstore. Point, click, and *"that's the title I'm looking for."* And Amazon succeeded. The errand to the bookstore became a time-consuming and costly burden compared to getting online, clicking a title, and clicking to check out. With the use of algorithms, Amazon could anticipate your desires as a customer, recommend your next purchase—and watch this, now—suggest a personal course for you to acquire more.

When Bezos speaks of *having my creativity and technological vision bear fruit and change the world in a positive way,* it's not necessarily only convenience and the shopping experience he has in mind.

In marketing books, and then eventually launching publishing platforms for independent voices—those whom traditional publishing wouldn't touch—Amazon deconstructed and then reconstructed the entire publishing world with one gate—theirs.

Amazon paved the way to e-commerce. They can also be credited with starting a migration from books in print to digital books. With the arrival of the Kindle in 2007, the world's readers experienced another sea change. Amazon had created—and monopolized—another market: knowledge in bytes. A decade on (at the time of this writing), all other comers in the digital book reader arena still lean heavily on Amazon for content to be viewed on their devices.

The gatekeeping example mentioned earlier, Amazon's decision to remove a conservative author's work from a bestseller list because of a few—granted a very loud and persistent few—complaints, cannot be taken lightly.

In his book, Ryan Anderson considers recent developments in our society in popular culture, law and medicine that have changed American opinion on gender identity, and presents both the views of transgender activists and those who believe gender cannot be severed from biological sex.[12]

He articulates that people need to respect the dignity of those who identify as transgender but argues against encouraging children to undergo experimental transition treatments. Under what lens does that qualify as hate speech?

> Amazon's decision to remove a conservative author's work from a bestseller list because of a few complaints cannot be taken lightly.

It's not as if Anderson's position is extreme. "The best biology, psychology, and philosophy," he notes, "all support an understanding of sex as a bodily reality and of gender as a social manifestation of bodily sex. Biology isn't bigotry."

Yet, the audacity with which Anderson and his book have been opposed, one could argue, is bigotry.

Anderson concludes, "Transgenderism is a belief system that increasingly looks like a cultish religion . . . being forced on the public by the state." Aided and abetted, it appears, by the new gatekeepers.

CHAPTER 4

Facebook: "Move Fast and Break Things"

"Instead of building walls, we can help build bridges."

—**Mark Zuckerberg**, Co-Founder and CEO, Facebook

Do you remember life before Facebook? Millennials don't. On the surface, it appears to be a place where people connect; where everyone can speak their mind and express their individuality. It is a participatory medium in contrast to television and radio, in which users passively watch and listen. Facebook invites you into the action; invites you to interact, act, and react. Because it is participatory, Facebook is empowering. Read, think, and express your opinion. Your audience awaits. Facebook founder Mark Zuckerberg has said it himself, *"Our goal is to give everyone a voice."*

But is that really what is happening?

Facebook is, in reality, a platform of evolving rules and procedures for posting, viewing, and interacting with information. While they proclaim to be "giving everyone a voice," these rules and procedures were devised by Facebook for Facebook's benefit. And Facebook is constantly monitoring its users, auditing your every Facebook interaction, friends, and interests. Most disturbing, while Facebook gives the impression it liberates users to really be themselves, it's actually employing the data it collects to nudge users in directions it deems best. Freedoms . . . hacked.

Mark Zuckerberg and a few college friends launched Facebook in his Harvard dorm room in 2004. It started as a Harvard-only thing, a means of meeting and connecting with other students. It soon expanded to include other area college campuses, then colleges everywhere, and then to all people, everywhere. Quite literally, Facebook became a global community. Just a few years in, Zuckerberg—still in his twenties at the time—was named one of the world's 100 wealthiest and most influential people.

And Facebook? Numbers (most of them from 2017) read like this:[13]

- There are 2.13 billion monthly active Facebook users.

- 1.40 billion people on average log onto Facebook daily and are considered daily active users.

- 1.15 billion are mobile daily active users, on average.

- Facebook 'Like' and 'Share' buttons are viewed across almost 10 million websites every day.

- Every 60 seconds 510,000 comments are posted, and 293,000 statuses are updated.

- 300 million photos are uploaded to Facebook every day.

- More than 4.75 billion items of content are shared daily.

- One-in-five internet page views each day are Facebook views.

These numbers are eye-popping. With those kinds of numbers comes tremendous power—and Zuckerberg knows it. "In a lot of ways Facebook is more like a government than a traditional company. We have this large community of people, and more than other technology companies, we're really setting policies."[14] That last sentence is worth re-reading.

> With those kinds of numbers comes tremendous power—and Zuckerberg knows it.

Before there was Facebook, there was a sharp kid growing up in White Plains, New York. Zuckerberg began using computers and writing code when he was in middle school. One of his childhood friends recalled, "Some kids played computer games. Mark created them." A model student, he transferred to the exclusive private school Phillips Exeter Academy in New Hampshire in his junior year. There he won awards in math, astronomy, and physics. With quite an impressive academic résumé, he graduated from Phillips Exeter Academy in 2002 and headed to Harvard. He dropped out of Harvard in his sophomore year.

> Call him a computer programmer or an internet entrepreneur, but Zuckerberg thinks of himself as a hacker.

Call him a computer programmer or an internet entrepreneur, but Zuckerberg thinks of himself as a hacker. You hear that expressed in statements he's made over the years, such as, "It's okay to break things to make them better," and one of Facebook's early mottos, "Move fast and break things." The company, in its early days, regularly held hackathons—events where they'd provide music, food and beer, and have a group of hackers in and spend a night creating. "The idea is that you can build something really good in a night," Zuckerberg said. "And that's part of the personality of Facebook. It's definitely very core to my personality."

Facebook's power is in its algorithms. As we've seen with Google and Amazon, Facebook develops algorithms to automate thinking, remove decisions, and *move people*. Also, like the others we've considered, their algorithms and their aims are shrouded in secrecy. They are supposed to be scientific and removed of all bias, but as we have seen before, algorithms reflect the beliefs of their creators.

When a platform's algorithms suggest some content over others—perhaps deciding recent articles are more important than older articles—or leaning in one direction over others—deciding a scientific answer is of more benefit than a spiritual answer—are they really scientific and unbiased? When we outsource our thinking to technology, we are really outsourcing our thinking to the companies controlling the technology—and we do so at our own peril.

We briefly considered the inconsistency of Facebook determining a Christian website's statement that *homosexuality and abortion are sin* violates the platform's *standards on bullying and hate speech*, while determining a group named for its desire to *find the author of a pro-life blog* and *"burn whoever runs it alive"* is not bullying or hate speech.

Find the Activist Mommy and burn her alive—is that not a threat? Is that not harassment or bullying? Is that not a possible incitement for violence?

Although the folks at *"I Will Find the Activist Mommy and Burn Whoever Runs It Alive"* were cleared by Facebook, they did, of their own accord, subsequently change the title of their group. One can only assume they wised up—having a death threat in your title must pose a legal risk. Now they're known as *"May God Make the Activist Mommy Spontaneously Combust."* Is that any better? Although the title no longer levels a specific death threat, isn't publicly wishing for someone's death some form of harassment and bullying?

Warriors for Christ, the site mentioned earlier, banned for violating Facebook's community standards on bullying and hate speech, labels themselves as "a ministry unapologetically opposed to all sinful behavior." When Facebook blocked their page, they had some 225,000 followers. Although they post on a litany of topics—marriage, adultery, fornication—yet it is the mention of homosexuality that triggers complaints. Those posts are routinely flagged for offensive content. "We can't even use the term 'LGBT' in any context whatsoever," said Pastor Rich Penkoski, "or else it immediately gets flagged and banned. If we type those four letters out on our page, it gets removed."

When Penkoski's page was taken down, he received this message from Facebook:

> *Your Page "Warriors for Christ" has been removed for violating our Terms of Use. A Facebook Page is a distinct presence used solely for business or promotional purposes. Among other things, Pages that are hateful, threatening or obscene are not allowed. We also take down Pages that attack an individual or group, or that are set up by an unauthorized individual. If your Page was removed for any of the above reasons, it will not*

*be reinstated. Continued misuse of Facebook's features
could result in the permanent loss of your account.*

"We have never done anything close to that," Penkoski says. "In fact, we have stated emphatically that we don't want harm to come to anybody, whether they agree with us or not. Our job is to preach the truth because we want people to live better lives."[15]

To be clear, the point of this exposé is not to either justify or vilify particular messages or messengers. It's about *gatekeepers* and our *rights to free speech and expression.* When a platform and its policies can determine one groups' expressions are *hateful, threatening, or obscene* while another's are acceptable, simply based on who is offended by them, we have cause for concern.

This is only the tip of the iceberg.

> When a platform and its policies can determine one groups' expressions are hateful, threatening, or obscene while another's are acceptable, simply based on who is offended by them, we have cause for concern.

Julio Severo is a Brazilian writer and blogger who maintains a site called Last Days Watchman. Its masthead reads, "Bringing you articles by a man who has felt God's call to alert God's people in these last days." His site is populated with articles covering a number of topics, many of them covering political or social issues, all interwoven with his spiritual take on them. In January of 2018, he penned an article entitled "*Why Does Facebook Harass and Censor Christians?*"[16]

In the article, Severo shares about his own tumultuous experience with the gatekeeper. He'd been notified by Facebook that he's been blocked from posting for 30 days—and this was the third or fourth time it had happened to him—because he'd violated their community standards.

Specifically, Facebook pointed to two articles, one on homosexual groups taking advantage of Brazilian taxpayers' money, and a second on Norway's efforts to deport Muslim criminal immigrants.

Severo's story is even more intriguing because of the timing. These two stories for which he was blocked were posted in 2013 and 2014. *In other words, Facebook reached back four and five years, culling his content, for something with which to silence him.* "With this latest block, using old posts," Severo charges, "Facebook is clearly showing that conservative views are not tolerated in its environment. It is showing that it has no willingness to give users safety and freedom for conservative views."

And Severo contends, the articles in question contain "no improper language or personal attacks." He explains, "If they read my exposé on the homosexual movement in Brazil, they'd conclude this document is journalistic and professional, just denouncing how homosexual groups abuse Brazilian taxpayers' money. On Norway's deporting Muslim criminals: If Muslims rape and commit other crimes in Norway, can they not be deported? Can I not report their deportation? Can I not support Norway's efforts to deport Muslim criminals?" Apparently not on Facebook.

Ironically, Severo feels as if he's the one being harassed and bullied. "Even when there are no direct blocks on my account, my comments and interactions on Facebook have been treated as spam and deleted. People are often blocked from sharing my posts. It is shadow banning. This is Facebook censoring, harassing, and bullying me for my conservative Christian stances."

It's not just shutting down sites and banning content that has people concerned. It's that *giving everyone a voice* claim. Facebook's *everyone* doesn't really mean everyone.

Severo's Last Days Watchman recently published a story about New York State Assemblyman Dov Hikind (D-Brooklyn). Hikind noted that while creating a profile, Facebook gives users 50 nationality options. The options, he claimed, include Palestine but Israel is conspicuously absent.[17]

"Palestine is not even a country," said Hikind. "How did it end up as an option? Well, we all know the answer to that. Facebook should stop its shameful exclusion of Israel."

In a December 2015 post on his Facebook page, Mark Zuckerberg spoke out in support of Muslims "in our community and around the world" who were being persecuted for the actions of others, in the aftermath of the Paris bombing. In voicing his support, he explained, "As a Jew, my parents taught me that we must stand up against attacks on all communities."[18]

Assemblyman Hikind points to Zuckerberg's own words as doublespeak. "The exclusion of Israel from Facebook, a publicly traded company, while Palestine is included is no accident—it's a purposeful, racist insult that must be addressed immediately."

Magdi Khalil is an Egyptian-born human right's activist, now an American citizen, residing in Virginia. He's been a well-known commentator on Middle Eastern affairs; made more than a thousand TV appearances as a political commentator on Middle Eastern TV channels; published articles and research; and authored several books. Khalil has founded several human rights centers and is presently the director of the Middle East Freedom Forum.

Given Kahlil's advocacy for human rights and the rights of religious and ethnic minorities in the Middle East, he's attracted the attention and hostilities of Islamic extremists. His Facebook page has become a target, and his account is regularly flagged as offensive.[19]

"In August 2016, I called for a peaceful march in front of the White House in defense of oppressed Christians in Egypt," Khalil explains. "Following that announcement, my account was hacked." The hackers altered his page to reflect ISIS ideology and threats. The FBI was alerted. It took ten days for the page to be restored.

In November 2017, he posted an article calling for religious reform in the Middle East. The article was deleted by Facebook administration and his ability to post was suspended for several days, despite the fact that this was an opinion article, and didn't include any call for hatred or violence.

In December 2017, it happened again. Another opinion piece on religious reform—article removed, privileges suspended, this time for two weeks.

In February 2018, Khalil posted another piece, this one expressing his opinion of Turkey after its military campaign in the north of Syria. This time, the piece was removed, and his account suspended for 30 days.

Khalil wants to know how this can happen. "I am a U.S. citizen, protected by the U.S. Constitution. Nothing I have posted, since I first signed up for my Facebook page, violates U.S. laws or Facebook rules. This falls under the freedom of opinion and speech, which is protected by the First Amendment to the Constitution of the United States, as well as by international laws and human rights instruments."

Beyond the freedom encroachment, Khalil points out the duplicity with which Facebook's practices are applied. "As a researcher and human rights activist, I see, to my great amazement, thousands of pages on Facebook full of hatred and incitement to violence against Christians, Jews, and women in the Middle East. These pages are left undisturbed, while Facebook Administrators go after a human rights activist for posts written in support of human rights and freedoms, and to counter global terrorism which poses a threat to the whole world."

"I left Egypt to escape religious persecution and the restrictions that crippled my freedom to write and express my opinion," he says. "I would not have believed my free-

> I see, to my great amazement, thousands of pages on Facebook full of hatred and incitement to violence against Christians, Jews, and women in the Middle East.
>
> —Magdi Khalil

dom would be suppressed in the United States, the land of the free."

In February of 2016, we got a close-up look from the inside at Facebook's duplicity when a contract employee named Benjamin Fearnow took a screenshot of a company memo and passed it off to a journalist friend.[20]

Mark Zuckerberg penned the memo to all of Facebook's employees addressing something that happened in the company's headquarters. There is a wall on which members of the team are encouraged to scribble notes, and share quips and thoughts. On at least a couple of occasions, someone had crossed out a message which read "Black Lives Matter" and written "All Lives Matter" in its place. Zuckerberg's memo called on whoever was responsible to stop. Specifically, he wrote: "'Black Lives Matter' doesn't mean other lives don't. We've never had rules around what people can write on our walls. Crossing out something means *silencing speech*, or *that one person's speech is more important than another's.*"

Not long after sharing this memo, something else caught Fearnow's eye—another internal communique, this one requesting employees to vote on questions to be asked of Mark Zuckerberg at an upcoming company-wide event. Fearnow noted the most popular question read: *"What responsibility does Facebook have to help prevent President Trump in 2017?"* He screenshotted this one on his cell phone.

The algorithms and liberal-biased curators are determining for Facebook users—for you and me—What's fair? What's fact? What is most important for us to see?

Fearnow worked in Facebook's New York office on Trending Topics, a feed of popular news items that pops up when people open Facebook. The feed is generated by—you guessed it—an algorithm, but it's moderated by a team of people with backgrounds in journalism. If the word "Trump" was trending, as it often was, this team used *their judgment* to identify which bits of news about the candidate were most important. Couple *using their judgment* with the aforementioned *most popular question*, "What responsibility does Facebook have to help prevent President Trump in 2017?" and let this sink in: *The algorithms and liberal-biased curators are determining for Facebook users—for you and me—What's fair? What's fact? What is most important for us to see?*

The day after Fearnow took the second screenshot—it happened to be his day off—he was summoned to a teleconference with three Facebook employees, one of whom was the company's head of security. He was fired, told to close his company laptop and not to reopen it.

In the aftermath of the 2016 presidential election, Facebook is revising its policies governing what appears in news feeds, prioritizing user content over publisher content, and prioritizing content that's acted upon. This appears to simply be another way to censor views that don't jive with Facebook's values.

Mac Slavo of Freedom Outpost wrote, "Facebook told publishers that content from reputable publishers will also be surfaced. It didn't specify how it would define 'reputable publisher' or how their traffic would be impacted, though. The worry for publishers is that such an approach will have the unintended consequence of hurting high-quality content because a lot of legitimate news articles, while they may get read, tend not to get shared or commented on."[21]

> This appears to simply be another way to censor views that don't jive with Facebook's values.

The Daily Sheeple's Joe Joseph put it into laymen's terms for his audience. "Let me rephrase [what Facebook told publishers] for people just so we don't use the term 'fake and offensive content.' It's any content that Facebook says it doesn't like. That's what this is. It has nothing to do with fake or offensive. *It has everything to do with anything Facebook doesn't like or perhaps runs counter to narrative and worldview."* [22]

As this new iteration of Facebook's policing policy took effect, Yale University researchers published a February 2018 study claiming to mirror Facebook's sorting of "broadly trusted" news sources from "partisan" sources. The study listed far-left sites like Salon and Huffington Post as "broadly trusted" and labeled right-of-center news organizations as "hyper-partisan." [23]

The study reveals that media sources are likely to gain "broadly trusted" ratings simply because of name recognition. CNN, NY Times, HuffPo—people know them. Newer and less familiar sources struggled to make the trusted column in the study.

> The study reveals that media sources are likely to gain "broadly trusted" ratings simply because of name recognition.

Admittedly, this Yale University study seems to mirror Facebook's new policies. What we can say is that if Facebook's methodology for determining "broadly trusted" news sites is similar to the one used in this study, then it is likely to inflate the trustworthiness rankings of mainstream news networks, many of whom are the least trusted in America.

Then there's this—Facebook's incessant experimentation and tinkering within their platform and algorithms, and their studying *you*. Recall from earlier, Facebook has boasted "knowing" its users. Zuckerberg has suggested they can predict users' race, sexual orientation, relationship status, and drug use *all simply based on "likes" alone.*

In his book entitled *World Without Mind: The Existential Threat of Big Tech*, author Franklin Foer includes a hypothetical scenario spun by Harvard law professor Jonathan Zittrain. [24] With all we have considered to this point, ponder this possibility:

There's a down-to-the-wire election and Mark

Zuckerberg has a strong opinion about the candidate he would like to prevail. Facebook claims it can boost voter turnout by placing reminders of civic duty in news feeds on Election Day, generating social pressure to head to the polls. This, by the way, isn't just a public relations claim, but an established finding of social science. Imagine—Facebook launches another get-out-the-vote campaign, only this time the reminders are placed selectively. Facebook has a good sense of your political persuasion based on all the items you've liked. They also know your demographic, and they know your location—or more specifically your voting precinct. Instead of urging all citizens to perform their civic duty, Facebook calibrates its call to action to target only those voters likely to pull the lever for Zuckerberg's preferred candidate.

We have our heads in the sand if we think this hypothetical can't become—or isn't already—reality. The responsibility of guiding the public to information is a sacred trust. In whose hands have we placed it?

CHAPTER 5

Apple: "Think Different"

"Our whole role in life is to give you something you didn't know you wanted. And then once you get it, you can't imagine your life without it. And you can count on Apple doing that."

—**Tim Cook**, CEO, Apple

CENSORED

Founded in 1976 and incorporated a year later, Apple was a player from the start of the personal computer revolution. What started as sort of a niche computer manufacturer has grown to become the world's largest information technology company. In 2015, Apple became the first U.S. company to be valued at over $700 billion. The company employs more than 123,000 full-time employees, maintains 500 retail stores in 22 countries, and operates the iTunes Store, the world's largest music retailer. Apple reported annual revenue of $229 billion for fiscal year 2017.

Apple's rise in the computer technology race can be traced to its users' ferocious brand loyalty. But its rise to media supremacy can be traced back to an advertising campaign that redefined the music industry forever: *Rip. Mix. Burn—After all, it's your music.*

We have been making the case that these tech giants are benefitting from the popularity of their new media platforms to control and shape our thinking. But they are not just controlling and shaping our thinking, they are also using their control to shred the value of their competitors' products so that they can monopolize them. Apple's conquering the music industry is, perhaps, the clearest example of this value shredding/hostile takeover practice.

> What started as sort of a niche computer manufacturer has grown to become the world's largest information technology company.

For example—the greatest selling musical album of all time is *Thriller* by Michael Jackson. It will never be unseated. Never. It's not that another talented artist won't come along who could rival the king of pop's talents, song-writing, and performing prowess. It's just that albums are a thing of the past, cast upon the scrap heap of entertainment media devices. They're old school. Apple ushered in a new day for music consumers. The future is in selling singles.

The music industry was brought to its

knees. Consumers quit buying albums for $18 when they could buy single songs off the albums for $1. And, with the devices available— and Apple started that ball rolling, too, with its initial iPods—now your entire library of music could fit and be carried about in a device the size of a matchbox. Add earbuds and . . . go. That rip, mix, burn campaign addressed the music that consumers already had in their CD collections. Apple Music allowed you to rip songs off those discs, mix them into playlists as you so choose, and burn them to your devices. Take all your music with you—everywhere. After all, *it's yours.*

From there, music piracy became easier than a hop, skip, and jump. Why not borrow and rip your friend's music? Why not create websites where ripped music can be shared? Why not make bootlegging a new digital pastime—and very lucrative pastime—for techie kids? After all, it can all be yours.

At the time the original iPods—digital music storage and playing devices able to hold thousands of songs—were being developed, Steve Jobs and his team could have made them block pirated music. While Jobs spoke against piracy, his device afforded users a license to steal. It was by design—*push the music industry to the brink and then take it over.*

This is about more than changes to the music industry. This is about intellectual property and artistic ownership, co-opted, and now controlled by Big Tech. If you're an artist and you want to get your music to your audience, you now need to play by Apple's rules. If your music isn't listed on iTunes, your boat is pretty much dead in the water.

And that's how they do it.

We briefly considered a case of Apple censoring Human Coalition, a Pro-Life group, by dropping their five-star rated app from their App Store. That instance was brought on by the concentrated effort of a group of liberal bloggers conspiring to pepper Apple with complaints about the app.

What is so offensive? The app contains a feature called "Prayer Feed" that offers a real-time map where others are praying. Users can swipe to confirm they are praying for someone considering an abortion.

"Harnessing the power of prayer and technology, this Prayer App brings together praying people from across the country in real-time for one purpose: to pray for abortion-determined families as they walk through their decision process," reads the description of the app.

Its real offense is that it upset a small group of liberals, and thereby moved Apple to act.

Apple wasn't entirely honest with Human Coalition in their explanation. "In July, on the heels of pro-abortion media pushback," the group says, "Apple notified us that they removed the Human Coalition app from the App Store, citing violations of certain functionality requirements. However, Human Coalition spoke with Apple and demonstrated that not only were the cited requirements met, but that the Human Coalition app exceeded minimum requirements and functioned better than similar apps from other developers."

Brian Fisher, co-founder and president of Human Coalition, shared his appraisal of the move with Fox News: "There is a growing trend in the U.S. to attempt to deter or silence Americans who oppose the fatal discrimination against preborn children. This move by Apple is not surprising, though it is a deep disappointment. Human Coalition remains committed to providing compassionate, loving care to women and their children even in the face of these challenges."[25]

For the scope of this exposé, we've looked only at the big four—Google, Amazon, Facebook, and Apple. But know this—the tentacles of digital censorship run far deeper and wider. Here are a handful of additional examples:

- Twitter blocked U.S. Senate candidate Marsha Blackburn's ad because it contained this sentence: "I am 100 percent pro-life. I fought Planned Parenthood, and

we stopped the sale of baby parts."
A Twitter representative told Blackburn's campaign that statement was
"deemed an inflammatory statement that is likely to evoke a strong
negative reaction.[26]

> Just about every social media platform has stories of flagging, blocking, and removing content considered offensive—based on the political and ideological views and leanings of those who control these platforms.

- Twitter shuttered Live Action's pro-life ads, finding photos of ultra-sounds of babies in the womb as offensive and inflammatory. Planned Parenthood, meanwhile, is allowed to advertise abortion services on the platform, uncontested.[27]

- Former Milwaukee County Sheriff David Clarke had his account temporarily suspended on Twitter after publishing a series of posts calling out media bias. Clarke was forced to delete the tweets in order to have his account restored.[28]

- Twitter, meanwhile, allows Minister Louis Farrakhan's Twitter account to continue unchecked, in spite of his statements railing against whites and Jews.[29]

- YouTube (owned by Google) is censoring the educational videos of conservative radio host Dennis Prager's PragerU with titles such as *The Most Important Question about Abortion, Is Islam a Religion of Peace?* and *The World's Most Persecuted Minority: Christians.*[30]

Just about every social media platform has stories of flagging, blocking, and removing content considered offensive—based on the political and ideological views and leanings of those who control these platforms. Many claim they are "tolerant," but in reality they are only tolerant of views that align with their own. Anything that calls their positions into question or advocates for deeper dialogue is considered "hateful" and "harassing."

So, what's at stake? And what can we do about it?

YOUR FREEDOMS—IN THEIR CROSSHAIRS

CENSORED

Consider this timeline—it is far more representative than exhaustive:[31]

- November 2010—Apple removed Chuck Colson's Manhattan Declaration from its iTunes App Store.

- July 2012—Facebook temporarily removed Gov. Mike Huckabee's post in support of Chick-fil-A.

- October 2012—Facebook removed Special Operations Speaks PAC's post critical of President Obama's handling of the Benghazi attack and put a 24-hour block on their account.

- January 2013—Facebook removed a post by Chicks on the Right that was critical of the White House press secretary, citing a violation of its Statement of Rights and Responsibilities.

- July 2013—Facebook removed a post and temporarily blocked the account of Fox News commentator Todd Starnes which spoke favorably of the NRA, Chick-fil-A, Paula Deen, Cracker Barrel, the Gaithers, and the Gideon Bible, citing violations of its Community Standards. (Also that summer, Facebook suspended the account of a UNC-Wilmington professor making arguments against same-sex marriage, as well as the account of a group called Military with PTSD, citing its Community Standards.)

- December 2013—Twitter blocked users from linking to a petition supporting Phil Robertson, who was suspended from the Duck Dynasty television show on A&E after voicing his Biblically-based views on homosexuality.

- October 2014—Twitter blocked users from linking to a petition supporting Houston pastors whose sermons were subpoenaed by the city because they supported a referendum against a city ordinance that would allow men in women's bathrooms in the name of providing protection for sexual minorities.

- April 2015—The crowd-sourcing site GoFundMe deleted fundraising campaigns for Sweet Cakes by Melissa and Arlene's Flowers, two small businesses that had declined to provide services for same-sex marriages. GoFundMe changed its terms of service to support its decision.

- November 2015—Facebook blocked postings by Vanderbilt University professor, Dr. Carol Swain, after liberal student activists organized complaints about her religious and moral viewpoints.

- November 2015—YouTube terminated the account of Olive Tree Ministries after they posted an interview about the persecution of Christians in the Middle East.

- May 2016—Gizmodo, a technology blog, reported evidence of Facebook workers censoring conservative content and injecting preferred articles into its influential trending news feed.

- July 2016—YouTube temporarily blocked a Center

for Security Policy video critical of the Muslim Brotherhood, Jihad, and Sharia Law.

- October 2016—Prager University announced that Google's YouTube was censoring many of its educational videos by placing them in "restricted mode," which flags and prevents them from being accessed freely.

- March 2017—Vimeo removed 850 videos produced by the Pure Passion TV citing disagreement with the ministry's views on sexuality.

- August 2017—YouTube demonetized hundreds of videos produced by Dr. Michael Brown, host of Line of Fire radio show, citing controversial religious content.

- January 2018—YouTube flagged and deleted the live stream of NRBTV for an unspecified Community Guidelines violation. YouTube also imposed a three-month block on NRBTV's account.

We at D. James Kennedy Ministries aren't immune. In January 2017, Amazon denied us access to its charitable AmazonSmile program based on our categorization by the SPLC as "an active hate group."

These companies are the most powerful gatekeepers of information and knowledge the world has ever known. They have taken control of the markets and mediums where they function and are setting up hierarchies of information to which they control access. Their platforms are

These companies are the most powerful gatekeepers of information and knowledge the world has ever known.

constantly spying on us; using information about our likes, choices, aspirations—even our friends—to push us in directions they want us to go. They are laying waste to our privacy and pressing us into a frightening conformity. They are linking arms with others who share their worldview, conspiring together to silence dissenting voices. They're blurring the lines between fact and fiction and mainstreaming misinformation. Their so-called "objective" algorithms are doing the heavy lifting of removing choices, thinking, and deciding for us. These tech giants aspire to mold humanity into their desired image of it. Furthermore, while it is happening right under our noses, we have been oblivious to it all. *Point. Click. Repeat.*

> These tech giants aspire to mold humanity into their desired image of it.

But no more! It is time to recognize what is happening, to understand the ramifications, and to take a stand for liberty's sake.

First of all, take the tech giants at their very own words—and carefully consider the implications of what they say when you do:

> *Our whole role in life is to give you something you didn't know you wanted. And then once you get it, you can't imagine your life without it. And you can count on Apple doing that.*
> —Tim Cook, Apple CEO

> *If we were motivated by money, we would have sold the company a long time ago and ended up on a beach.*
> —Larry Page, Google Co-founder, Alphabet CEO

> *Nothing influences people more than a recommendation from a trusted friend.*
> —Mark Zuckerberg, Facebook Founder & CEO

In the postmortem of the 2016 election, many observers determined social media—Facebook and Twitter, in particular—added wind to Donald Trump's sails, especially in those traditionally blue states, Wisconsin, Pennsylvania, and Michigan, which ultimately closed the deal for him. It seems as if these social media platforms agree, which is no doubt fueling the changes they are implementing. As 2018 dawned with an important ballot of mid-term battles on the horizon—Facebook's CEO, Mark Zuckerberg, shared with the platform's users his decision concerning a shift in practice:

One of our big focus areas for 2018 is making sure the time we all spend on Facebook is time well spent.

We built Facebook to help people stay connected and bring us closer together with the people that matter to us. That's why we've always put friends and family at the core of the experience. Research shows that strengthening our relationships improves our well-being and happiness.

But recently we've gotten feedback from our community that public content—posts from businesses, brands and media—is crowding out the personal moments that lead us to connect more with each other.

It's easy to understand how we got here. Video and other public content have exploded on Facebook in the past couple of years. Since there's more public content than posts from your friends and family, the balance of what's in News Feed has shifted away from the most important thing Facebook can do—help us connect with each other.

We feel a responsibility to make sure our services aren't just fun to use, but also good for people's well-being. So we've studied this trend carefully by looking at the academic research and doing our own research with leading experts at universities.

The research shows that when we use social media to connect with people we care about, it can be good for our well-being. *We can feel more connected and less lonely, and that correlates with long term measures of happiness and health.* **On the other hand, passively reading articles or watching videos—even if they're entertaining or informative—may not be as good.**

Based on this, we're making a major change to how we build Facebook. **I'm changing the goal I give our product teams from focusing on helping you find relevant content to helping you have more meaningful social interactions.**

We started making changes in this direction last year, but it will take months for this new focus to make its way through all our products. The first changes you'll see will be in News Feed, where you can expect to see more from your friends, family and groups.

As we roll this out, you'll see less public content like posts from businesses, brands, and media. And the public content you see more will be held to the same standard—it should encourage meaningful interactions between people.

For example, there are many tight-knit communities around TV shows and sports teams. We've seen people interact way more around live videos than regular ones. Some news helps start conversations on important issues. **But too often today, watching video, reading news or getting a page update is just a passive experience.**

Now, I want to be clear: by making these changes, I expect the time people spend on Facebook and some

53

measures of engagement will go down. **But I also expect the time you do spend on Facebook will be more valuable. And if we do the right thing, I believe that will be good for our community and our business over the long term too.**

At its best, Facebook has always been about personal connections. **By focusing on bringing people closer together**—*whether it's with family and friends, or around important moments in the world*—**we can help make sure that Facebook is time well spent**— Mark Zuckerberg's Facebook post of January 11, 2018.[32] [Emphasis added.]

Note, first of all, Zuckerberg's assumption that he and his Facebook team should determine what makes for "time well-spent" by Facebook users, and that gathering information by reading news or watching a video is a "passive" experience, and therefore not "time well-spent."

Also, amidst all of Zuckerberg's high-sounding rhetoric is a subtext, according to conservative talk-radio icon Rush Limbaugh. "The subtext is that it will decrease visibility to pages run by publishers and news sites. Consider this: at the inauguration of President Trump, Fox News' coverage attracted the most viewers on cable news—an average of 8.8 million. **But their Facebook video of the same even attracted almost twice that number: 16 million.**"[33] [Emphasis added.]

So, for all of the seeming idealism about changing from "helping you find relevant content to helping you have more meaningful social interactions" and doing the right thing for the good of "our community" (and let's not forget—for Facebook business too), ultimately, it is more *censorship*, more limits on what you the Facebook user will be allowed to see, and more shaping of your thinking by limiting your reading and viewing options.

In another example of these tech giants rushing to double down on their content filtering efforts, Alphabet/Google announced plans to add 10,000 new staffers tasked with tracking down *extremist* content on YouTube.[34] This is the company that chose *Snopes, Climate Feedback,* and *the SPLC* to help them fact-check content already. How do you suppose the SPLC will help them define *extremist*?

All of it, no matter the policies, procedures, and politics they employ, is an affront to our freedoms, especially our freedom of speech.

> All of it, no matter the policies, procedures, and politics they employ, is an affront to our freedoms, especially our freedom of speech.

Since these Big Tech companies are private entities, they are not subject to the same sanctions that would protect our First Amendment rights if they were government agencies. As Robert Verbruggen points out in his article, "Our Digital Overlords," in *National Review*:

> To be clear, this does not pose any sort of First Amendment issue—these are private companies, and the Constitution does not dictate how they program their search algorithms or decide which stories appear on users' news feeds. But the potential for political meddling is substantial and troubling when a single company controls a key way that Americans across the political spectrum find their information.[35]

That scenario has already been discussed in chapter four. Clearly our government should have some concerns when four tech monopolies have, as Verbruggen points out, "an extraordinary power to shape public discourse."

It will no doubt take time before these issues are sorted out in ways that protect both individual privacy, personal freedom of expression and speech, and non-interference with the political process. However, there are some actions, which we can take as individual believers, that can move the discussion in a positive direction and even guide the decision-making of those who have the power to effect changes in this arena. In the final chapter, we will share steps and actions that we can take to defend our individual freedoms.

CONCLUSION

WHAT CAN WE DO?

You have read this exposé because you believe in *standing for truth* and *defending your freedom*. You realize we cannot remain idle on the sidelines. What can you do? First, recognize that what is at stake is our freedom of speech and religious expression—the freedom to tell people who we are, who Jesus Christ is, and what we believe. Then, we need to take action—to take a stand for freedom and our religious liberty.

Earlier, we considered American Freedom Defense Initiative President Pamela Geller's website disappearing from Google searches, being denied access to AdSense, and having her PayPal account suspended because of complaints by liberal activists and because she had been deemed a hatemonger by the SPLC.

She has since spoken out, criticizing senior Facebook executives for assuring the government of Pakistan that "Facebook will enforce sharia by blocking explicit, hateful, and provocative material that's critical of Islam."

"It's extraordinary that the West is succumbing, submitting, to this really most extreme ideology," she said. "Will it happen? It is happening. We need legislative action on Facebook, on Google—the crushing of free speech."

We considered Tennessee Republican Marsha Blackburn's experience of Twitter censorship during her campaign. One week after the FCC rolled back the Obama-era "net neutrality" regulations, Rep. Blackburn introduced HR 46882, the Open Internet Preservation Act, in the House of Representatives, along with 21 co-signers. The issue of Big Tech censorship is getting the attention of members of Congress.

As this was going to press, Facebook CEO Mark Zuckerberg

was testifying before Congress concerning the use of data of 87 million Facebook users by outside agencies. Sen. Ted Cruz used the opportunity to say, "Mr. Zuckerberg, I will say there are a great many Americans, who I think are deeply concerned that Facebook and other tech companies are engaged in a pervasive pattern of bias and political censorship." He went on to cite "numerous instances" of such censorship including shutting down the "Chick-Fil-A Appreciation Day" page, and blocking Trump supporters Diamond and Silk, who had 1.2 million Facebook followers.[36]

In addition, the Federal Trade Commission is investigating Facebook. Three dozen state attorneys general have asked for more information, and the Illinois Attorney General has filed a lawsuit accusing Facebook of breaking the state's consumer fraud law. The lawsuit states:

> Though it may have started as a social network, Facebook's business model has shifted over the years into what is now one of the biggest data-mining companies in the world . . . **Facebook now uses its platform . . . to manipulate users into making the decisions that Facebook and its business partners want them to make.**[37] [Emphasis added.]

Others are taking note of the way the new gatekeepers are manipulating those who use their services. Now is the time to take action. Our voices must be heard. We must use our voices, our resources and our resourcefulness, our prayers and our petitions to support efforts to defend free speech. The following are ways we can do so:

- Track these and other efforts to address gatekeeping and censorship.

- Let your elected officials hear from you.

- Contribute financially to organizations like D. James Kennedy Ministries, or any of the other organizations shining light on efforts to censor Christians and conservative voices.

- Support the production and airing of the upcoming D. James Kennedy Ministries national TV Special, *Censoring the Truth: Facebook, Google, and the New Media Gatekeepers*, which will help inform and involve people across the country.

- Be selective in your own use of social media and your media consumption.

- Support those voices and entities that are doing it right.

- Get creative—pen an op-ed, share relevant posts, call a talk show—let your voice be heard.

- Help expose more people to what is happening and encourage them to get involved.

- Pass a copy of this book along to your pastor and friends at church.

- And *do* pray—don't just say you will—*do it*. Make this a matter that you bring before the throne of God.

Google, Amazon, Facebook, Apple—and other tech providers—simply cannot be allowed to function as gatekeepers of ideas and content—especially in ways that prevent the Gospel from having free course.

Big Tech believes they know what's best for us. That has always been the way of those who would censor and silence ideas they dislike and positions they oppose. History has shown over and over that the first step to tyranny of any kind and any degree begins with the shutting down of freedom of speech and free sharing of ideas. On the other hand, when these freedoms prevail—as was the case during the Protestant Reformation and later during the founding of America— religious freedom flourishes and leads the way for nations to prosper and thrive, and for the Gospel of Jesus Christ to have free course.

> Let us resolve to do everything in our power to retain our freedom of religious free expression on these new media platforms that God may use us and them to spread the liberating message of freedom in Christ—in ways "yet undreamed of"—so that the good news of the Gospel may be proclaimed throughout the Earth, introducing people to the Person and the redeeming work of Jesus Christ.

ENDNOTES

1   Franklin Foer, *World Without Mind: The Existential Threat of Big Tech,* (New York: Penguin Press, 2017), 4-5.

2   Pamela Geller, "Facebook Shuts Down 'Warriors for Christ' Page," *Geller Report,* January 1, 2018, https://gellerreport.com/2018/01/facebook-warriors-christ.html/ (accessed March 28, 2018).

3   Megan Fox, "Group Threatening to Burn 'Activist Mommy' Alive Doesn't Violate Standards, Facebook Says," *PJMedia,* January 16, 2018, https://pjmedia.com/trending/group-threatening-burn-activist-mommy-alive-doesnt-violate-standards-facebook-says/ (accessed March 29, 2018).

4   Eric Lieberman, "Google's New Fact-Check Feature Almost Exclusively Targets Conservative Sites," *The Daily Caller,* January 9, 2018, http://dailycallercom /2018/01/09/googles-new-fact-check-feature-almost-exclusively-targets-conservative-sites/ (accessed March 28, 2018).

5   Perry Chiaramonte, "Apple Censored Pro-life Group by Dropping App, Activists Say," *Fox News,* October 17, 2017, http://www.foxnews.com/tech /2017/10/17/apple-censored-pro-life-group-by-dropping-app-activists-say. html (accessed March 28, 2018).

6   Ariana Eunjung Cha, "Ryan Anderson's Book on Transgender People Is Creating an Uproar," *The Washington Post,* February 2, 2018, https://www.washingtonpost.com/news/to-your-health/wp/2018/02/02/ryan-andersons-book-calling-transgender-people-mentally-ill-is-creating-an-uproar/?utm_term=.20aee9b05a29 (accessed March 28, 2018).

7   Franklin Foer, op. cit.

8   Richard L. Brandt, *The Google Guys: Inside the Brilliant Minds of Google Founders Larry Page and Sergey Brin.* (New-York: Portfolio-Penguin, 2011).

9   Eric Lieberman, op. cit., 3.

10   Kevin Daley, "Lawsuit Claims Rank Internal Bias at Google, Sweeping Commitment to Identity Quotas," *The Daily Signal,* January 11, 2018, https://www.dailysignal.com/2018/01/11/lawsuit-claims-rank-internal-bias-at-google-sweeping-commitment-to-identity-quotas/ (accessed March 28, 2018).

11   John Hayward, "Pamela Geller: Too Much Power over Free Speech in the Hands of a Small Number of Big Tech Companies," August 24, 2017, *Breitbart,* http://www.breitbart.com/radio/2017/08/24/geller-power-free-speech-hands-small-number-big-tech-companies/ (accessed March 28, 2018).

12   Ryan T. Anderson, *When Harry Became Sally: Responding to the Transgender Moment,* (New York: Encounter Books, 2018).

13   "The Top 20 Facebook Statistics - Updated March 2018," Zephoria Digital Marketing, March 14, 2018, https://zephoria.com/top-15-valuable-facebook-statistics/(accessed March 28, 2018).

14   David Kirkpatrick, *The Facebook Effect: The Inside Story of the Company That Is Connecting the World,* (New York: Simon & Schuster Paperbacks, 2010), 254.

15   Samuel Smith, "Facebook Takes Down 'Warriors for Christ' Page Citing Policy on Bullying, Hate Speech, *Christian Post*, January 9, 2018, https://www.christianpost.com/news/facebook-takes-down-warriors-for-christ-page-citing-policy-bullying-hate-speech-212992/ (accessed March 29, 2018).

16   Julio Severo, "Why Does Facebook Harass and Censor—Block—Christians?" *Barbwire*, January 21, 2018, https://barbwire.com/2018/01/31/why-does-facebook-harass-and-censor-block-christians/(accessed March 28, 2018).

17   Julio Severo, "Facebook Excludes Israel and Includes Palestine," Last Days Watchman, February 8, 2018, http://lastdayswatchman.blogspot.com/2018/02/facebook-excludes-israel-and-includes.html (accessed March 28, 2018).

18   Mark Zuckerberg, December 9, 2015, https://www.facebook.com/zuck/posts/10102517406079831(accessed March 28, 2018).

19   Magdi Khalil, "Facebook 'Intellectually Terrorizes' a Human Rights Activist," *Frontpage Mag*, February 20, 2018, https://www.frontpagemag.com/fpm/269363/facebook-intellectually-terrorizes-human-rights-magdi-khalil (accessed March 28, 2018).

20   Nicholas Thompson & Fred Vogelstein "Inside Two Years That Shook Facebook—And the World," *Wired,* February 12, 2018, https://www.wired.com/story/inside-facebook-mark-zuckerberg-2-years-of-hell/ (accessed March 28, 2018).

21   Mac Slavo, "Facebook Says Big Change Is Coming: 'It's Time To Pull Out All The Stops Of Censorship,'" SHTFplan.com, January 18, 2018, http://www.shtfplan.com/headline-news/facebook-says-big-change-is-coming-its-time-to-pull-out-all-the-stops-of-censorship_01182018 (accessed March 28, 2018).

22   Ibid.

23   Allum Bokhari, "Yale Researchers Accidentally Expose Facebook's Bias Against Conservative Media," *Breitbart,* February 8, 2018, http://www.breitbart.com/tech/2018/02/08/yale-researchers-accidentally-expose-facebooks-bias-against-conservative-media/?utm_source=facebook&utm_medium=social (accessed March 28, 2018).

24   Franklin Foer, *World Without Mind: The existential threat of Big Tech*, (New York: Penguin Press, 2017), 123.

25   Perry Chiaramonte, "Apple Censored Pro-life Group by Dropping App, Activists Say," *Fox News,* October 17, 2017, http://www.foxnews.com/tech/2017/10/17/apple-censored-pro-life-group-by-dropping-app-activists-say.html (accessed March 29, 2018).

26 Susan Berry, "Twitter Allows Abortion Ads, Blocks Pro-Life Messages as 'Inflammatory,' 'Offensive,'" *Breitbart*, October 10, 2017, http://www.breitbart.com/big-government/2017/10/10/twitter-allows-abortion-ads-blocks-pro-life-messages-inflammatory-offensive/ (accessed March 28, 2018).

27 Ibid.

28 Madeline Fish, "Twitter Temporarily Suspends Sheriff David Clarke's Account Over Tweets Assailing Media," *Fox News,* January 2, 2018, http://www.foxnews.com/politics/2018/01/02/sheriff-david-clarkes-twitter-account-temporarily-suspended-over-tweets-bashing-media.html (accessed March 28, 2018).

29 Joseph A. Wulfsohn, "Twitter Would Rather Punish Conservative Steven Crowder Than Anti-Semite Louis Farrakhan," *The Federalist*, March 19, 2018, http://thefederalist.com/2018/03/19/twitter-rather-punish-conservative-steven-crowder-anti-semite-louis-farrakhan/ (accessed March 29, 2018).

30 Mat Staver, Holly Meade, and Matt Barber, "PragerU Files Federal Censorship Lawsuit Against YouTube (Audio), *Barbwire*, November 14, 2017, https://barbwire.com/2017/11/14/prageru-files-federal-censorship-lawsuit-youtube-audio/ (accessed March 28, 2018).

31 "Timeline: Documenting Online Censorship," *Internet Freedom Watch*, (n.d.), https://internetfreedomwatch.org/timeline/ (accessed March 28, 2018).

32 Mark Zuckerberg, January 11, 2018, https://www.facebook.com/zuck/posts/10104413015393571 (accessed March 28, 2018).

33 "Google Wins 1, Loses 1 in Major Court Rulings," *WND,* March 27, 2018, http://www.wnd.com/2018/03/google-wins-1-loses-1-in-major-court-rulings/print/ (accessed March 28, 2018).

34 Tim Brown, "YouTube Hires 10,000 Brownshirts To Rid You Of 'Extremist' Content," *Freedom Outpost*, December 7, 2017, https://freedomoutpost.com/youtube-hires-10000-brownshirts-rid-extremist-content/ (accessed March 28, 2018).

35 Robert Verbruggen, "Our Digital Overlords: Big Tech Is Becoming a Problem," *National Review*, December 18, 2017, 29-32

36 Ian Schwartz, "Zuckerberg to Cruz on Bias: Silicon Valley "Extremely Left-Leaning" Place, "I Understand" The Concern, *RealClearPolitics.com*, April 10, 2018, https://www.realclearpolitics.com/video/2018/04/10/zuckerberg_to_cruz_on_bias_silicon_valley_extremely_left-leaning_place_i_understand_the_concern.html (accessed April 11, 2018).

37 Stephen Dinan, "Facebook Under Fire as Prosecutors, Congress Confirm Investigations," *The Washington Times,* March 26, 2018, https://www.washingtontimes.com/news/2018/mar/26/facebook-under-fire-prosecutors-congress/ (accessed March 28, 2018).